POCKET GUIDE TO
MEDITATION

ALAN L. PRITZ

The Crossing Press • Freedom, CA

For information on bulk purchases or group discounts for this and other Crossing Press titles, please contact our Special Sales Manager at 800/777-1048.
Visit our Web site on the Internet: www.crossingpress.com

Library of Congress Cataloging-in-Publication Data
Pritz, Alan.
    Pocket guide to meditation / Alan L. Pritz.
        p. cm. -- (The Crossing Press pocket series)
    Includes bibliographical references.
    ISBN 0-89594-886-9 (pbk.)
    1. Meditation--Handbooks, manuals, etc. I. Title.
II. Series.
  BL627.P75   1997
  291.4'35--dc21   97-26037
                                  CIP

I dedicate this to the Divine through Whom I have been blessed with a wonderful spiritual master, Paramhansa Yogananda, a very special wife, Deborah, my ever-loving parents, Benjamin and Louise, and my most amusing brother, Neil.

Many thanks to Cathy Bronakowski and Jim Vetsch for their editorial insights and effort.

My additional appreciation to the staff at The Crossing Press for their wonderful help and assistance with this project.

CONTENTS

Preface

This book is for anybody interested in meditation and spiritual growth. If you are one of the vast numbers of people hungering for a deeper connection with Spirit, read on.

Meditation is a universal tool. Many people feel an intuitive comfort with the idea of meditation. In my experience, however, they are occasionally put off by its cultural associations, New Age or Eastern. I want to remove this obstacle by providing classical information about meditation in a fashion and language that Westerners can apply to their own culture or religious heritage.

Introduction

For over twenty-five years I have studied and taught meditation, yoga, and martial arts. Professionally, I extract principles from these disciplines for performance enhancement and lifestyle management trainings for various businesses and health care organizations. The purpose of this book is to go one step further and provide some nuts-and-bolts information about the art and science of meditation as it applies to spirituality in everyday life. Nothing in this book is really new. The information is essentially timeless and has been shared by those far wiser than myself. I have been strongly influenced by the teachings and works of Paramhansa Yogananda. The book, a rendering of the works of others filtered through my experience and perceptions felt like it wanted to be written, so I am obliging it. In following my muse, hopefully there will be some novelty of presentation that is beneficial or inspiring.

One principal reason for writing this book stems from the resurgent interest in spirituality evident in the great flood of "new age" materials and books about angelic encounters, near death experiences, and related phenomena. Much effort has been expended looking for new expressions, new forms, new visions, and new interpretations of spirituality. However, aside from the rising interest in Buddhism, there has been scant information focusing on the merits of classical spiritual practice. Little has been written to explain clearly and sensibly the scientific rationale behind meditation. Perhaps people have blindly followed spiritual dogma for so long that they forget to question the validity of spiritual practices. Whatever the reason, meditation makes sense. There are justifications for its practice that offer insight into the sometimes vague process of spiritual development.

To convey why spiritual practice and meditation are so necessary in these modern times, I draw from the classical tradition of yoga as taught by Paramhansa Yogananda. The word "yoga" means "to unite." Its practice focuses on uniting the consciousness of the individual or soul to Infinite Consciousness, Spirit, or God. Not a religion in itself, yoga looks at spiritual development scientifically much the way modern medicine details the nature and function of our physiology. In yoga, meditation becomes central to inner discovery. Anyone can benefit from its practice regardless of religious affiliation. Rather than compromising or threatening traditional or personal spirituality, meditation deepens an individual's relationship with the Divine.

Many people may find so much attention to Spirit uncomfortably foreign at first. Others may really be looking for simple coping skills or ways to relax. I honor these experiences, but I'd be doing meditation a grave disservice if I diluted it for marketing purposes. Relaxation exercises, while they are excellent for inner stability and also function as a preparation for mediation, are not meditation and should not be considered as such.

My sincerest wish is that people begin to explore their spirituality more deeply. Those who feel the pressures of global change can easily appreciate why. We live in an age of tremendous technological potential and need to harness these outer resources with balanced inner development. To assist in that process and to make spiritual principles a bit more understandable, I've used information drawn from my years of study and experience. I hope to convey this material in a way that's both motivating and fun, intelligible and interesting.

For those restless to begin an actual meditation practice, simply skip to the last chapter. Keep in mind, however, that the information provided along the way is designed to explain the process as well as get you started.

What Is Spirituality?

Spirituality seems as if it ought to be easy to understand. In ancient Greece the package was relatively straightforward. Human beings were composed of three parts; body, mind, and spirit. Of course the Greeks were never mentally lazy and therefore began wondering about how these parts fit together and whether body and mind were separate from spirit, etc. So, as usual, intricate theories developed as did endless talk, dialogue, and dispute.

Later in the late 20th century we have a veritable smorgasbord of agendas. Look at what we rant about now! Was Jesus gay? Was he black? Did he really even exist? What can we dig up about Moses, Krishna, or Buddha? (Better steer clear of Mohammed). Do Native Americans, Aborigines, or other indigenous/shamanistic traditions really have "The Answer"? A feast of political, sexual, esoteric and paganistic "isms" all strive for expression and identity. It's all become so terribly territorial, mind numbing, and externally focused that many common, fundamental truths seem almost irrelevant.

Spirituality will inevitably mean different things to different people. This is to be expected. Without telling people what to think, I will present some of my insights and opinions for consideration. If anything rings true, try living it for yourself.

Spirituality is a basic part of us, as intrinsic to human nature as our bodies and minds. Actually, more so. We can do without a limb or two, perhaps even lose a few thousand brain cells, but we can't get by without our spiritual self. It is the most fundamental aspect of who we are, the building material of our bodies and minds, the stuff of life. To live or work in any capacity disconnected from our spirit is to forfeit the mystery and meaning of who we are and what life is all about. It's like walking on a sunny, warm beach wearing army boots—you're there, but you just don't get it.

Spirituality is not to be confused with religious affiliation. We've all known sanctimonious types who regularly attend religious services and activities, yet love to damn others who don't tow the line. Such fervor is really lip service and has nothing to do with spirituality. Rather, spirituality is the essence of all traditions, the Truth hiding behind and within every form. It is the medium through which individuals establish a direct communion with God, regardless of formal orientation. Spirituality is both the immediate experience of That-Which-Is-Holy, the Higher Power by whatever name, and living by those principles and practices which foster this relationship.

I submit that we all hail from a common origin in Spirit. Vast beyond human intellect and rational comprehension, this Source transcends every dogma. That various forms of worship exist in the world today simply reveals the diversity of approaches to our Essential Nature. To assume otherwise, that we could somehow limit the Infinite, is almost laughable. After all, it's difficult enough for most of us to understand the workings of a car engine or VCR much less the mysterious origins and subtle operation of the universe. This isn't to say that anything goes or that Absolute Truth is relative. Far from it. The spiritual realizations of enlightened beings like Jesus, Krishna, Moses, Buddha and Mohammed complement each other. Having transcended ordinary human consciousness, they perceived reality with Divine vision, directly and accurately. Consequently, their teachings reflect the same eternal truths.

An important point to address early on is the tendency for dogmatic individuals to advocate only one true spiritual path and teacher. Such attitudes, which I term spiritual youthfulness, lack broader understanding. Those of such limited vision are often so entrenched in their religious world view that they don't, can't, or won't see the larger picture. A wonderful parable captures this point vividly:

> An elephant owner assigned each of his 5 blind children to wash a part of the animal. When done, the kids began fighting over their different experiences. One, assigned to wash the tail, described the beast as rope-like. Another thought the elephant was like a tree for she washed its legs. A third, who washed the sides, said the elephant was like a huge wall. And so on. Hearing the commotion, the father laughingly broke up the dispute explaining they were all correct, but not complete in their descriptions. Being blind they couldn't see the whole animal and fought over their limited, vested insights.

Buddha taught about karma, the law of cause and effect. Jesus taught "As ye sow, so shall ye reap." Buddha emphasized right living to overcome suffering and attain salvation. Jesus preached winning heaven through love, grace, and righteousness. Yet when I mention such similarities, someone will inevitably want to focus upon the seeming differences. And surely there are certain differences. Yet doesn't this remind you of the blind children and elephant parable? Such a minute focus obscures the big picture. Think about it. Doesn't teaching first grade differ from teaching high school? Of course it does. And isn't home economics different than geography? Obviously. Likewise, spiritual teachings reflect the cultural and spiritual needs of different peoples at different times. The common goal of these teachings, however, no matter how unique or specialized, is to move people towards the same end: reunion with the Divine.

Perhaps looking at an alleged difference between two great world religions will be insightful. For example, let's briefly target the basic Christian doctrine that Jesus is the sole savior of mankind, the one and only route to redemption. According to John 14:6-7, Christ said, "I am the Way, the Truth, and the Life; no man cometh unto the Father but by me...If ye had known Me, ye should have known my Father also; and from henceforth ye know Him, and have seen Him..."

To question whether this is meant literally or figuratively is unthinkable for some and heresy for others, and also the route to a painful demise or tormented eternity for many others. But what about the identical but differently worded claims Bhagavan Krishna makes about Himself? "I am the Aum (Pranava) in all the Vedas, the Sound in the ether," he says in the *Bhagavad Gita*, the Hindu bible, (7:6-8). "I make and unmake this universe. Apart from Me nothing exists...All things like the beads of a necklace are strung together on the thread of My consciousness, and are sustained by Me." So there you have it, two traditions seeming

to claim a divine monopoly. Not surprisingly, the funda-
mentalist sects in both groups consider each other heathens.

While I don't mean to get sidetracked with scriptural
interpretation, let's think about this for a moment. These
comments about singular divine status though they are
quite straightforward and still misunderstood. The truth is
both Jesus and Krishna are correct. Jesus wanted people, if
they could, to understand His teachings on a deep spiritual
level, not just in a literal manner; "He that hath ears to hear,
let him hear," he says in Luke 8:8. This is a classic miscon-
struing of an esoteric meaning for a superficial one.

Neither Jesus nor Krishna referred to their divinity
in terms of the limited human personality or individual
body, i.e. as "Sons of Man." They, like other fully awakened spiritual masters, successfully scaled the peaks of
Self-Realization and spoke from a reference point of
God-consciousness. Both could rightfully claim kinship
or oneness with Spirit. Neither of these spiritual leaders
claimed exclusive divine privilege, but instead demonstrated a level of spiritual attainment each of us is privy
and entitled to. Jesus for instance, when challenged about
His divinity, responded to accusers in John 10:34, "Is it
not written in your law, I said, Ye are gods?" And John
1:12 reads, "But as many as received Him, to them gave
He power to become the sons of God." Likewise Krishna
told His devotees, "Absorb thy mind in Me...so in truth
do I promise thee; thou shalt attain Me." (*Bhagavad Gita*
18:65) These are hardly pronouncements of monopoly.
Rather, they're testimonials to supreme generosity.

The "Him" and "Me" referred to by Jesus and
Bhagavan is the "Son of God," the single voice of universal

Christ/Krishna consciousness, the prodigal soul child returned to oneness with Spirit. It's not about singular physical bodies.

Ultimately, it's not our capability to discuss these matters that is important, but, our ability to experience them fully and directly for ourselves that counts. That's what all the Great Ones have made available for us. Such is the very reason, the very heart, of spiritual practice.

This is what meditation is all about.

What Is Meditation?

Periodically I'll meet a child who asks, "What's meditation?" This usually stops me in my tracks. I can talk *ad nauseam* to adults or even teenagers, about the spiritual mysteries of consciousness, but to a kid? What's so wonderfully refreshing about this kind of encounter is the simplicity of response it evokes: Meditation teaches people how to be happy. That's it. Of course, there's a lot more to it which we'll explore later in this book, but the beauty and power of meditation isn't something sensational. It simply delivers one of the most purely profound experiences of life, joy.

Why is this so important? We all yearn for joy. It's a fundamental human drive to seek that which gives joy and to avoid that which causes pain. But we seldom analyze what joy is, why it's significant, or where it comes from. Instead, much of our time is spent banging into walls of materialism; chasing money, careers, relationships, toys of every kind in a passionate search for pleasure and security. Such effort is really a misguided attempt to connect with joy. This feeling, however, is never found outside ourselves and is definitely not an ingredient of things. That we experience pleasure in association with objects merely shows we're capable of tapping into that response. The joy itself does not come from external sources but from within us, in our responses. It is a quality of Spirit and belongs to our essential nature, which is joy. Thus in Spirit alone is the fulfillment, the happiness, the joy that we seek.

Meditation is of greatest value because it connects us directly to this inner joy. It quiets the mind, opens the heart, and allows us to receive Divine consciousness. Neither a blanking of the mind nor a "fluffy" contemplation is a spiritually rapt state of mind.

In common parlance meditation means the practice used to attain spiritual immersion. It is the spiritual science of retracing our steps back to the Godhead and at its most advanced levels, meditation imparts union with the totality of Spirit. Savants of divine realization say that in such states the soul melts back into Spirit. Consciousness, formerly identified only with the physical body, unites with God in superconsciousness and expands to embrace all creation and the mysteries beyond in an ecstasy of boundless love, peace, and bliss. This is the consummate goal of meditation and the highest attainment of human potential. It's here we find our true Home. The Buddhists call it Nirvana. The Hindus, Samadhi. For Taoists, The Source. And for Christians, Salvation: "Him that overcometh will I make a pillar in the temple of my God, and he shall no more go out." (Revelations 3:12) Being fashioned from Spirit, we are kin to the Sacred. It is our divine birthright, therefore, to acknowledge and claim the truth of Jesus' words, "Ye are gods."

There's no patent on this universal tool. Spirit is equally available to us all. Most religions have some form of meditative discipline with which to find God within. Consequently, it's not uncommon for saints of different faiths to share similar mystical experiences. St. Theresa of Avila for example, a renowned Catholic saint from the Middle Ages, described going into ecstasy as having her soul shot like a bullet from the base of the spine to the crown of her head, exactly how yogic adepts describe a "kundalini-awakening" experience. This commonality suggests that our spiritual natures spring from one source and are not subject to relative interpretation. Just as we each have bodies with blood, bone, and muscle, we also have common spiritual components. Likewise we all share a similar purpose in our sojourn on Earth and have a common final destination in Spirit.

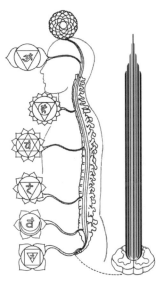

This is rather staggering. Although we reside in the world, we are not of it. Our nature is something far greater, eternal, and infinite. If we truly embrace this concept, then we must also adjust our way of thinking and behaving. This is the challenge of modern times, to grow into the 21st century with an operating paradigm based on spiritual realities and not simply financial ones. Thus our platform for daily interaction must change from narrow self-interest to a broader vision of common humanity. To live accordingly requires an attitude of mutual cooperation and compassion. Everyone becomes family, and all countries home. This doesn't mean we stop all activity and join the nearest hermitage. We must learn to balance external achievement and economic prosperity with inner development. By doing so, we contribute to the harmonious evolution of humanity and foster the highest potential in us all.

Meditation for
Times of Change

Living in a world of paradox and relativity isn't easy. Divorced from a higher context and without some form of inner anchor, people lose purpose and perspective. Life becomes a random, temporary existence with no greater purpose than earning fat incomes and buying toys. The obvious results of this attitude are greedy materialism, unhealthy self-indulgence, and gloomy bumper stickers declaring "Shit Happens!" A world built upon such a shoddy structure is destined to collapse.

A glimpse at the world today illustrates this all too clearly. Tremendous upheaval, conflict, and senseless brutality are evident on many global stages. In the face of this, one may ask how meditation fits into the picture. Is it a magic wand to remove crime from inner cities, to restore world peace, renew the environment, or eliminate greed and corruption? No. It is a means towards such an end. Meditation serves as a viable tool for transformation, a vehicle to enable us to experience the spiritual fabric of ourselves and all other beings. By so doing we can gradually learn to live in a manner both positive and uplifting.

One positive effect of current global crises is that they prompt us toward a renewed search for personal meaning and spirituality, and they increase our desire to invest meaning and spirituality in our personal and professional activity.

Widespread chaos shows that no single person, race, sex, or religious group is responsible for our panorama of problems. The issues before us reflect the collective thoughts and actions of individuals made over time. These can be addressed and resolved only through the choices we each make hour by hour, day to day. How? Our individual attitudes and behaviors must change. We need to reject actions of darkness, selfishness, and violence. We need to reclaim the ethics and values which foster light, compassion, and peace. To change ourselves, therefore, is the most potent way we can uplift and help others. Meditation fosters such change and provides the direct, ongoing spiritual experience to sustain it. This rediscovery of ourselves in a larger spiritual context may truly be the only way we as a society, country, and world community can survive and thrive.

Even the Western medical community has begun exploring spiritual paradigms, prayer in particular, for healing purposes. Larry Dossey, MD concluded in his book, *Healing Words: The Power of Prayer and The Practice of Medicine*, that we do exist on levels more subtle than the physical, and that spiritual power, when properly applied, is a definite beneficial force. While this is nothing new to some of us, the medical establishment is signaling a new respect for spiritual practice.

How else is spirituality practical? Spiritual laws exist and operate regardless of our beliefs about them. For those who apply them, they work. Would a farmer doubt that seeds, once planted, will sprout given proper conditions? No. Is the farmer a simpleton for believing in that process? Again, no. Why not embrace our own spiritual reality, harness it for our greatest good? Instead of resisting spiritual principles and practices let them benefit our lives?

If the powerful business community begins to under-stand the value of spirituality and taps into the practice of meditation, the creative decisions and actions arising from such a "higher" perspective will be both organizationally rewarding and globally enhancing. This isn't meant to reduce meditation to a commercial level, but rather to advocate including spiritual guidance and vision in every aspect of our lives.

Peace and Potential
in the Workplace

Many people may view meditation and the principles it embraces as too esoteric or other-worldly to be practical. Yet nothing could be further from the truth. Let's just look briefly at the incremental impact of our busy near-millennium lifestyles. My wife, a family-practice physician, sees numerous patients whose primary complaints or ailments are a direct result of stress. Studies corroborate that anywhere from 50–75% of physician visits are stress-related. That's an astounding number! Small wonder that Prozac™ and Xanac™ are the drugs of choice for the '90s.

Consider the financial impact of such stress on the business community. For years we've experienced a transitional economy because of the rapid technological advancement and its mixed blessings. Computers, while simplifying life in certain areas have complicated it in others. Increased production capabilities have wrought increased management expectations. Employees caught in the crossfire between technology and transition have had to face lay-offs, job restructuring, and/or greatly increased responsibilities. These circumstances and changes have generated deflated morale, decreased performance, heightened absenteeism, and a lot of stress.

This same work force is also increasingly sensitive to the impact of global strife, social issues, and ecological concerns.

People know that traumas like regional famines, political upheavals, and cultural devastations would not exist if we set our principles before our pocketbooks. Mixing heightened social concern with a shaky economy produces a work force ready for significant change. But this is hardly news. What is pertinent from a business perspective is the bottom-line impact that daily stress and social tension have upon employees. It has been medically proven that mental states affect physical health and well-being. Social scientists have shown that attitude influences performance. Therefore, can we expect unhappy or sick persons to do their best? Not for long. Are decreased morale and performance, increased absenteeism and health-care expense cost-effective? Hardly. Is this a recipe for longevity and prosperity? Probably not! What can meditation do to offset or eliminate these costly conditions? Select studies have shown that consistent meditation practice over time yields the following results:

- Stress reduction—Enhanced deep rest and decreased levels of generalized tension
- Decreased medical care costs—Improved health from stronger immune system
- Stimulation of cognitive ability—Increased intellectual and academic performance
- Improved morale—Increased energy, clarity, efficiency, productivity, job satisfaction
- Enhanced social behavior—Positive improvement in personality profiles
- Improved cardiovascular health—Lowered blood pressure

This demonstrates a tremendous, though largely untapped, personal and professional potential.

Our corporate cultures and environments must also change. We can't simply use meditation as a bandage applied over a dysfunctional system. Nor can we afford to think in isolated fiscal terms disregarding the financial impact of our actions on other societies. The effects of our vision and behavior are both planetary and long-lasting. Collectively our world possesses the technology capable of either re-creating or destroying itself. Simply put, we need to become a friendlier planet. Meditation can help do that.

Within the business world, professional development courses such as "Continuous Growth" and "Total Quality Management" programs are appropriate channels for investigating and implementing meditation-based trainings. In fact, although these movements have traditionally focused more on acquiring technology than cultivating human potential, some firms are currently exploring intuitive development to enhance creativity, develop leadership, and boost customer service. One example of this was the subject of a television documentary which revealed how a major corporation encouraged dream-monitoring to enhance employee problem solving and creative abilities. A staff engineer of the corporation used dream-accessed information to help solve a very costly industrial problem. Once he overcame some predictable skepticism from co-workers, his solution was found to be both viable and cost-effective.

A retired executive wrote to me about how meditation affected his life:

> I was led to meditation after a heart attack, a stroke, and open heart surgery. My cardiologist, a daily meditator himself, recommended it, and I used the method he employed…I made two 15-minute periods of daily meditation habitual—the first immediately after my morning shower and the second right after returning home from work, thus bracketing my workday with quiet time. The principal benefits were these:
>
> - I became a calmer person, mentally and physically. Workday stress was noticeably reduced.
> - My mind became sharper. Creativity and memory both improved.
> - I felt more in control of my life.
>
> I enjoyed a 36-year career with a wonderful company—Proctor & Gamble. It would have been even more enjoyable if I had learned earlier the value of meditation. I am thankful, however, that I was led to meditation in time to make the latter years of my career and the early years of my retirement better than they ever would have been without it.

While such training was not available to him at work, he sincerely wished it had been.

A humorous example of practical spirituality comes from a friend who is both a general contractor and minister. He uses spiritual inspiration and intuition throughout the workday to solve tricky construction problems, often finding solutions that have boggled others. He laughingly refers to these helpful ideas as coming from an invisible friend,

"Swami Fix-it"! Being present with the Divine, he claims, is a sure way to receive a steady stream of relevant aid.

The marketplace of life teems with stalls of duty, alleys of commerce, and halls of exploration. From mundane workaday matters to the most important life-saving ones, spiritual development helps people cultivate their fullest potential. Even a couple of testimonials hint at how such development can be tremendously beneficial. By harnessing the inner Self we are truly able to offer our very best. As the psychologist William James said, "The greatest revolution in our generation is the discovery that human beings, by changing the inner attitudes of their minds, can change the outer aspects of their lives." By developing our spiritual natures, we'll move beyond personal limitation and regional hardship into expansive awareness, collective abundance, and joyful harmony. It's our birthright to seek the kingdom within and our privilege to find it. May we rise to the challenge as we inherently deserve no less.

Stages of
Soul Development

Just as physical laws govern daily existence, more subtle ones govern spiritual development. Doubting such laws doesn't keep them from operating; they simply exist. For instance, an individual slipping from a ladder, regardless of personal beliefs about gravity, will fall. Mental acceptance is irrelevant to that reality. This also applies to metaphysical tenets and spiritual principles. Our private views and personal ideology don't negate the existence or operation of spiritual law.

By working in concert with these physical principles they can be applied for practical ends. Spiritual laws are no different. They reveal to us the hidden road map to higher consciousness and indeed declare that there is a higher reality for us to discover and reclaim. In order to find this higher ground however, we had better play by the book.

The fundamental tenet of a spiritual life is that existence has purpose, that it springs from a Divine Source and is not merely a random cosmic accident. Life has very real properties, meaning, and direction. That we lose sight of these doesn't change the reality. In fact, it amplifies the need to get back on track or suffer the consequences. This premise is vital because it provides an enduring spiritual context for why we are here and, more importantly, how to live.

The world is essentially a grand boarding school, and life is our school work. All experiences gained through living are multi-faceted lessons which serve to educate, entertain, and awaken us physically and spiritually. Just like passing through school, we progress through various life stages. We have lessons, homework, and tests. As we pass our tests, we get new assignments and gradually rise to higher life grades. This continues throughout our lives, and, according to the doctrine of reincarnation, over the spans of many lifetimes.

Eastern religions often use the lotus to symbolize this process. A gloriously beautiful flower, it begins life as a root in the muck at the bottom of a pond. Over time its stem grows upward through dim and murky water towards the light. Eventually breaching the water's surface, the blossom opens to the sun revealing its inner loveliness. We are like this, too. Originating  in darkness and ignorance, we can evolve gradually to shed selfish desires and base tendencies. Blossoming in the light of wisdom, love, and compassion, we can discover our true nature as Spirit and attain complete Self-realization. In unbroken divine communion we can fulfill our highest potential and graduate from our earthly training. Like Jesus, Krishna, Buddha, Moses, Mohammed, or other Great Ones, we can fulfill our divine legacy and return Home.

As mentioned earlier, Spirit is the fount of creation. It is also perfection itself and the ultimate manifestation of who we are. To reunite with spirit isn't self-annihilation, but the fulfillment of all longings and the quenching of all thirsts. Life obscures this fact so well that we must often endure a variety of painful experiences to learn to forsake material infatuation and seek happiness in the Divine.

Everyone's experience is unique leading to this quest. Some of my former clients give apt testimonials of this spiritual process. An accomplished attorney admitted that while outwardly successful, he felt disturbingly empty inside. His professional accomplishments were very flattering to the ego, but his inner self yearned for spiritual nourishment. Meditating became extremely important to him, and when last we spoke he was still practicing it. Another client, an airline pilot, had experienced a temporary depression and heightened anxiety arising from a health concern. It wasn't a serious condition, but it reminded him of his mortality. He thought meditation would help him find inner peace and perhaps overcome his dread of death.

Whether you know it or not, your life is a spiritual journey. Everyone is on the spiritual path, it's just a matter of degree. Some pursue it willingly, others don't. In the final analysis we all shall make the grade. It's merely a matter of time.

What are the rules for this journey, and how can we measure our progress? I will deal with the rules later as a natural lead-in to the section on meditation technique. As for measuring our progress, the value in this is not to foster a competitive outlook, but rather to heighten awareness of how we're doing and where we need help in order to improve our behavior and attitude. In a real school there are tests, report cards, and if need be, tutoring. In daily life we're lucky if friends give us candid feedback. Often we just suffer a series of hard knocks. This reminds me of a story:

> An Indian saint had a devoted group of followers but a very cantankerous neighbor. The neighbor continually faulted the saint for one thing or the

other, always laughing at the way people followed his every step, waiting to hear him speak. When eventually the neighbor died, the disciples joyously brought this news to their teacher. Much to their shock, the saint started weeping. Asked why he grieved the passing of this sour critic, the saint replied the neighbor had been a true friend, aptly pointing out faults and thus helping refine his character.

The point of appraisals is not to stroke our egos but to help us move forward, to refine our character. A cookbook approach to such evaluations, however, is tricky business. Everyone's spiritual saga is unique. Since we typically can't fully understand the mysteries behind others' circumstances, it's both unfair to judge them and unwise to make sweeping generalizations. Judgment is something best left to legal and "higher" authorities, yet discernment is valid to help us avoid repeating others' mistakes.

Having said all this, I offer this model for evaluating spiritual evolution and personal growth. I challenge readers to be honest with their observations of different kinds of human beings:

> Good, virtuous persons reflect archetypal qualities of love, kindness, courage, and compassion whereas people of ill repute demonstrate negative tendencies of deceit, cowardice, hatred, and violence.

These characteristics, though simplified, accurately depict refined or base qualities found in all people regardless of race, creed, color, or religion. It's a function of who they are on the inside.

Fortunately we're capable of improving ourselves, particularly through spiritual practice. As one sage put it, "Forget the past. The vanished lives of all men are dark with many shames. Human conduct is ever unreliable until man is anchored in the Divine. Everything in the future will improve if you are making a spiritual effort now."

This evaluative model originated in ancient India and chronicles the stages of spiritual awakening which culminate in illumination. These stages occur over many lives of increasing spiritual realization. The model's premise is that consciousness and life are evolutionary and people will manifest traits revealing their level of growth. For example, children with inordinate talent or wisdom beyond their years are considered clear evidence of prior lifetime development. This system can be applied in modern times, but I suggest some gentle discrimination. Certain insights are gems, yet they may be mixed with material you find unacceptable. Give it due consideration, take what feels true for you, and reserve judgment about the rest. According to these classical principles, the soul grows through four primary stages: The Root Phase, The Interactive Phase, The Selfless Phase, and The Transcendent Phase.

THE ROOT PHASE

In this very first phase, individual outlook is dominated by animal-like tendencies and passions. Consciousness at this level is extremely primal and self-centered, focused mostly on survival, power, and reproductive urges. To persons in this state, concepts of higher realities have neither practical purpose nor philosophic relevance. They want what they want when they want it, and their desires are primitive. Gradual upward development occurs, motivated by intelligent self-interest, when wants or needs appear best met through cooperative interaction. Like children who recognize that a lemonade stand can generate money for candy, basic self-interest gives rise to rudimentary service. As necessity is the mother of invention, so it is the catalyst for upward evolution.

Life provides increasingly complex challenges or lessons as people continue developing. Generating energy to meet those challenges taps undeveloped thought processes, emotions, and latent physical skills. In short, life stimulates expansion. Like metaphysical weights, life's struggles build moral strength and overall character. As one saint put it, "You don't get strong by wrestling babies." Interestingly, the famous vintner, Baron von Rothschild, spoke similarly about grapes, that adverse climates produced vineyards of superior refinement. Same truth, different applications. Yet how else do we learn except by experience? Who can develop compassion without suffering, or develop confidence without success? Each experience is a life lesson, but it's how we integrate and grow from such an experience that matters most. A popular bumper sticker says, "Those who finish with the most toys win." But I counter, "Those who finish with the *best character* win."

At the height of consciousness in this first phase, is the pursuit of material comfort and security.

THE INTERACTIVE PHASE

This phase introduces a second level of growth marked by a mature readiness to engage in cooperative interactions and social commerce. This isn't about promoting a work ethic, but about stepping beyond the island of basic ego. While most of us work from social necessity, few do so with drive and ambition. Many could care less. Seeing a universe broader than oneself, saying yes to life, truly reflects this expansion.

Surprisingly, this stage is often cultivated through business. Though free-market systems unfortunately reward greed and other base behavior, they also promote growth. People dependent upon government largess or centralized economies often become devitalized and void of creative spirit. Commerce enhances us because it stimulates individual resourcefulness and industry. Whoever wants success will pursue advanced skills, ensure quality, and provide superior service. Business communities reward these efforts, and they are natural settings for relevant growth experiences.

Work shouldn't be a drudgery, endured just to pay bills. When approached with the right attitude it's a privilege. To serve others is a gift. It fosters healthy self-esteem. Excluding occupations which cause harm or suffering, all work is good, none superior to another. It's ultimately not the specific duties, but how they're done, that counts. In this spirit, all honest work should be honored and performed with pride and gratitude.

The impact of business on workers has unfortunately turned negative in recent years, driving many dispirited persons to seek substantive change in their lives. By becoming increasingly profit-driven, self-serving, and amoral, our economic community has lost much integrity. This is one reason why there's such need for meditation training and the philosophies which accompany it. Perhaps this sounds self-serving, but consider the messages of three very popular old movies, *It's a Wonderful Life*, *Miracle on 34th Street*, and *A Christmas Carol*. They share themes of humanity that transcend commerce. They make us feel glad to be alive and want to do the right thing. I'll wager these cinematic visions are popular because people want to make them real, to recreate them in their daily lives. Wouldn't that be a wonderful life indeed? That so many recent movies don't offer this vision shows how far off kilter we've spun.

Fortunately the intrinsic good in people has a way of asserting itself like a moral immune system to reject what's unnatural and wrong. Increasing numbers of people want to renew the values that make work honorable and life enjoyable. This is particularly important in terms of spiritual growth because eventually intangibles become more valuable than personal or material gain.

THE SELFLESS PHASE

When our attention becomes drawn to service, local or otherwise, when the welfare of others becomes foremost in our thoughts, then we attain the third level of soul awakening, the phase of selfless service.

Such thoughtfulness is a great thing. It marks the transition from self-centeredness to expanded sensitivity and indicates great character. Even children receive praise or win gold stars for thinking of others. Selfless service is an advanced form of this virtue. Through honoring the divine in all, it evokes compassion and humility. By shedding self-importance, it fosters love for the great body of creation. Through purifying the heart of pettiness and bigotry, it builds bridges between all races and creeds. A good example of selfless service happened to me one day after work. I was grumbling on the way back to my car at the parking lot, when the attendant smiled at me with such heart-felt warmth and genuine goodwill sparkling in his eyes, that my blue funk simply vanished! Now that is selfless service. Nothing fancy, not the result of sophisticated training, simply the right attitude and right way of being. With self-less service our job doesn't matter, it's what flows through us to others that counts.

Varying degrees of selfless service exist. One can't become a Mother Theresa or Mahatma Gandhi all at once. The important thing is for the ego to become gradually transformed. The thick walls of narrow self-interest must erode until the Life Divine is felt within and amongst us all. Service to others then becomes service to one's own larger Divine Self. This is what Jesus meant when He said, "Thou shalt love thy neighbor as thy self" (Mark 12:31), and "Whosoever shall receive this child in my name receiveth Me." (Luke 10:48) We're all connected, children of the Divine. Even the animals and seemingly inanimate objects like rocks and soil are of Spirit. To ignore this truth is to deny reality. To live in accord with it is to embrace a kinder life. Only in this way can we hope to evolve as a people and a planet.

As we evolve in sympathy with others, it's natural to want to serve others and help ease their burdens. Yet a focus on social situations, no matter how worthy, ultimately pre-occupies us with mundane affairs. To a very real degree this is good and necessary. It refines us spiritually and makes the world a better place. Yet in the big scheme of things, life isn't about creating perfect societies. Have any great spiritual masters ever emphasized this? No. Why? Because worldly pursuits consume our attention and distract us from higher realities. Until we look beyond the fascination of external affairs to inner ones we shall remain estranged from our divine heritage. As Jesus said, "The kingdom of God cometh not with observation…for, behold, the kingdom of God is within you." (Luke 17:20-21)

It is said that suffering is good because it draws us closer to the Divine. Unfortunately, this is often true. Calamities have a way of triggering the search for spiritual meaning in life. They catalyze a craving for Truth and the need for answers to life's hidden mysteries. The external chaos forces us to look inside for stability and transcendence. This heralds a transition into the fourth and final leg in our journey of awakening.

THE TRANSCENDENT PHASE

At this stage we begin realizing that nothing but Spirit can provide the lasting satisfaction our soul seeks. A yearning for higher connection builds, and we develop an intense desire to unite with and serve the Divine. Worldliness, outgrown like old clothes, is gently laid aside. Selfless service is then transformed into serving the divine in everyone.

Some individuals at this juncture enter the ministry to concentrate on spiritual development. This reflects honorable intent and motivation but doesn't make them more holy than anyone else. People of the cloth are just as susceptible to human frailties and inappropriate behavior as anyone. What's important is not outer profession, but inner life, cultivating awareness of the Divine in everything, blending outer activity with inner communion/meditation. Learning to offer oneself, one's tasks, one's very life in complete surrender to the Absolute while functioning on a daily level builds spiritual maturity and greatness. And one needn't be a monastic to practice this. If everybody left society for spiritual obscurity, we'd have a crowded wilderness. Right attitude and consciousness are all that's necessary. In fact, one saint commented that becoming a millionaire is harder than finding God. He reasoned that the world has finite fiscal means so not everyone can become wealthy. However, as everyone has equal access to God, they're already halfway home.

Yet development even at this stage is evolutionary. Because someone yearns for inner fulfillment doesn't automatically make them Self-realized. In fact, upon committing to a spiritual path, people often find extra challenges and emotional or psychological baggage that need working through. This is a natural cleansing process just like clarifying butter. When heat is applied, impurities surface for removal. Our past wrongs and shortcomings manifest under the heat of acclerated soul development and are removed through struggle and growth opportunities. Eventually though, we reach such refinement that our spiritual efforts, augmented by Divine Grace, merit perfect awakening.

In Western Christian tradition, Jesus represents the pinnacle of this attainment. In the East, divine stature is deemed the birthright of every soul. Thus Buddha, Krishna, Rama, and others are equally revered. Considered fully illuminated, they all share complete spiritual union and assist straying humanity in regaining their divine legacy.

Understanding Oneness

A theme central to the practice and philosophy of meditation is that we are all essentially One. The image and language of oneness arises periodically in popular culture as in ecological contexts, but what does it actually mean? Furthermore, how does it affect us on a routine daily basis?

The totality of our personal and collective existence stems from Spirit. It was Einstein who suggested that the more he pondered the universe the more it appeared to operate as a play of infinite intelligence. In fact, the latest discoveries of theoretical physics support his conjecture. Ancient seers and yogis knew the world as Divine thought, a projection of spiritual force. They understood the subtle laws and workings of Divine consciousness, that ideas were created, energized, and ultimately condensed into matter. The entire universe emanates from and is sustained by Divine Will. It is a vast drama or grand, eloquent play of cosmic consciousness. We are one, because in truth, we're simply varied forms of a singular thing, Spirit.

Consider the individual realities we each create on a nightly basis in dreams. Using forms of internalized thought, our dream projections have all the elements of real experience to us. Thus a dreamer, while incorporating different elements within his/her dream, is still only using elements of consciousness. When we awaken from such experiences they are recognized as just dreams. The same principles hold true for television shows and movies. Regardless of the complexity of detail, drama, and so forth, in reality we only see projections of electrical light impulses upon a screen. In just this fashion our lives are also episodes projected from the factory of Divine consciousness.

Sound bizarre, or perhaps frightening? Who wants to think of themselves as nothing more than condensed thought? But all creation is this way and still very real to us. We now scientifically know that energy and matter are different forms of the same thing, but that doesn't change our daily life experience. Rather, such knowledge enhances our ability to manipulate matter and energy in ways previously unknown or inaccessible to us. If we take another step forward and embrace the idea that behind energy and matter lies consciousness, is that so far-fetched? We individually affirm this universal truth on a daily basis. Any time we create something we think of it first, then put energy into it, and eventually manifest it in physical form. Architects and builders do this all the time, as do all creative individuals.

The idea of being one in spiritual essence, but different in superficial form, should not be alarming. We don't lack individuality, awareness, or free will. These are divine attributes given to help us each realize our deepest spiritual nature. Awakened souls haven't just disappeared. After they have merged their consciousness with the Source of all existence, they continue to live and try to share the indescribable joy of the experience. Saints of various traditions have encountered this during periods of spiritual ecstasy. Even people recounting near-death experiences attest to feeling immense joy, purpose, and a sense of complete belonging to a loving Spirit or Godhead. Such incidents speak to the tremendous gladness we finally achieve in Divine Union. We should take comfort in this realization and further recognize that the projection of creation is done consciously and with love, not madcap whimsy.

Yet the concept of spiritual oneness amidst such diversity still seems quite a paradox. Having limited sense perceptions, we can see things only in terms of their individuality, not as part of a whole. Until the state of divine totality is experienced directly, not merely intellectually, we must live according to what we can sense. If we experience spiritual unity, however, then even tiny aspects of creation become meaningful. This, incidentally, is reflected in current ecological awareness and what has been taught historically by all great spiritual leaders. If one believes otherwise, that things exist without broader context, then only greed and disharmony result. With the former vision comes a lifestyle of compassion and respect. With the latter, a world of dog-eat-dog.

The next chapter's guidelines, based on universal principles, can make the concept of oneness a living reality.

Eight Steps Toward Divine Awakening

What is the best way to promote a spiritual life? Obviously each religious tradition has an ethical code to guide and measure daily conduct. Jews and Christians commonly share the Ten Commandments. Buddhists follow the eight-fold path of Dharma (Truth/Law). Hindus, Moslems, and other groups have similar frameworks. But how do we apply these to what's already been discussed? An East Indian saint once counseled, "Learn how to behave." His implication was more than simply that we have to be good. We have to understand and follow those guidelines which best help us attain the ultimate human goal, reunion with God. This requires both right action and proper understanding.

Doing something morally correct without necessarily knowing why is a form of good and right action. It demonstrates the intuitive element of conscience which distinguishes right from wrong. Yet acting without understanding can also be a form of blindness. Anyone can flick on a switch and have the lights turn on. But how many grasp the laws of electricity and can, like an inventor, direct them to desired ends? Spiritual practice should be like this, intelligent action done with reasoned understanding. It shouldn't be a matter of blind faith, but should make sense, if only from the perspective of a higher-law. For example, consider Christ's act of forgiveness from the cross. He had the power to destroy enemies with a thought, but acknowledged their spiritual ignorance instead. Understanding God as love, and seeking to awaken the divine within His persecutors, Christ accomplished far more through loving forgiveness than could ever be done by destructive force. Such is the power of spiritual law. It works, it endures, and it must ultimately be the building block of our daily affairs. And our essential spiritual oneness is at the heart of this law.

The yoga sutras form another ancient body of universal spiritual wisdom. "Yoga" literally means "to unite or yoke," and it is a spiritual science aimed at uniting the soul to Infinite Spirit. Its principles are based on the same eternal truths found in any true religion. Sutra means "thread," and it refers to the very essence of a teaching, one reduced to its most basic elements. Yoga specializes in quieting the mind, withdrawing attention from worldly influences, and uniting with God. The sutras describe how this process is accomplished most successfully and scientifically. Anyone using these skills to commune with the Divine, regardless of outer religious affiliation, can therefore be called a yogi.

For simplicity's sake, I'll not be going into all the yoga sutras. This would be cumbersome and would simply repeat the number of books on eastern philosophy or religion. Instead, I want to focus on the eight most pertinent steps needed to attain divine awakening. These eight stages provide the critical foundation and understanding necessary for an intelligent practice of meditation. That's essentially what this book is all about. Utilizing these steps will help the reader put meditation into correct perspective, and hopefully, into daily practice.

The first two of these eight steps contain ten fundamental guidelines for spiritual growth. Not unlike the Ten Commandments, these are universal do's and don'ts which prescribe qualities of mind and action required to promote spiritual consciousness and happiness. It's important to understand the individual guidelines in order to apply them properly. Since philosophical matters often make people fuzzy, the following insights are relatively short and sweet. The ten guidelines are like miners' tools which remove the darkness of ignorance covering the precious inner nature of our souls.

The fuel powering these tools is the recognition that underlying all the different forms of creation is one Spirit. In order to find God, behaviors which promote ego and separateness from the One must be forsaken, while those which foster harmony and unity need to be cultivated. These guidelines are goal oriented and indicate what must be embraced for success and avoided to prevent failure. As such, each guideline promotes a quality that deepens the realization of our true essential oneness.

STEP ONE: REMOVING OBSTACLES

The first step to divine awakening is comprised of five "don'ts" or "Nons"—guidelines to help us remove the obstacles to realizing our spiritual oneness.

- Non-violence
- Non-lying
- Non-sensuality
- Non-stealing
- Non-greed or Non-attachment

Non-violence

The first of these principles, non-violence, has obvious merit. It is clearly valuable to avoid physically harming others if only for purely social reasons. No one in their right mind would advocate wanton destruction. But non-violence is far from just a finger-wag against being brutish. Doing unto others as you would have done unto you is spiritually appropriate because others are a part of the Greater You. The idea that someone can be hurt without repercussion reinforces the lie of separateness. It denies the underlying law of spiritual unity. Thus harm done to any being also impacts the perpetrator. This principle extends even to how we think about others. Persons sensitive enough can actually feel mental criticism, judgment, or negativity directed towards them. Such negativity, besides being just plain nasty, poisons the minds of the ill-wishers, inhibits realization of the Divine in all, and erects walls of self-created darkness which ultimately lead to a lonely life of bitter isolation. The consciousness of non-violence, on the other hand, fosters an attitude of loving compassion that can transform even hardened enemies into supportive and enduring friends.

Non-lying

The second of these principles, non-lying, is also quite positive. More than simply not telling falsehoods, it refers to the necessity of weeding delusions from our garden of wishful fancies to get at the Truth. Fortunately, the Divine is not influenced by shifting human whimsy, pop psychology, or political correctness. What we think or want to be true may not be so. The spiritual path leads to "what is." This requires the moral bravery to examine our cherished opinions and discard whatever is false. Non-lying sharpens our spiritual perception which allows us to examine who we truly are, how we're behaving, and if we're moving closer to the Celestial Goal.

People often like to limit themselves by thinking, "I'm only human." They view personal, temporary faults as part of some inevitable, eternally flawed structure. I recently read a review about the character, Sir Lancelot, played by Richard Gere in the movie *First Knight*. The critic described Gere's performance as compelling because Lancelot was depicted as a man with a past who had nothing to lose. In other words, Lancelot wasn't exceptional for virtue's sake, but because he was running from ghosts. It's sad that virtue is no longer pursued or even understood for its own merit, but arises from another alternative.

Being human doesn't mean we're condemned to perpetual inadequacy. We have the potential for lasting greatness. Our divine reality is this highest potential. Non-lying insists that we abstain from a diet of self-loathing or, conversely, self-importance and feast instead on Truth. By claiming our divine birthright, we shed falsehood and polish our hidden natures. As John Anderson sang, "I'm just an ol' lump of clay, Lord, but I'm gonna be a diamond one day." And so can we all.

Non-stealing

The third principle, non-stealing, denounces the unlawful taking of others' property. But more importantly, it warns against the tendency to look outside the Self for happiness.

Stealing by its very nature focuses attention on external objects, affection, fame, whatever, as sources of joy. It represents the ultimate misdirection of our consciousness away from Spirit towards fulfillment in things, even those wrongly obtained. Non-stealing, however, helps free the soul from matter bondage. It affirms that lasting joy resides within us, that we can enjoy the marvels of creation without having to possess them. Further, we are children of a benevolent universe, and the more we harmonize with it, the more our needs are met without even asking. Stealing closes the mind to this realization while non-stealing opens it to absolute faith in our cosmic Self.

Non-sensuality

The fourth principle, non-sensuality, is a tricky one to explain and, frankly, a difficult sell to western audiences. The first thing crossing people's minds when they hear the term "non-sensuality" is, "What, no sex? I'm outta here!" So, rather than focus on sex and have people jump ship prematurely, let's try to understand non-sensuality in broader terms.

The essential theme repeated in all the guidelines so far has been to avoid anything that removes us from the complete center of Spirit within. In keeping with this, non-sensuality simply urges us not to seek lasting fulfillment through sense gratification. This can be best understood when we recognize that a basic component of our spiritual structure is energy. How much energy we possess and where it's directed impacts us on all levels. To grow spiritually, we must direct our energy to the center of divine perception residing in the brain. Success in this reaps lasting peace and joy.

Sensual indulgence, however, is a counterfeit joy broker. It diverts energy funds from the AAA-rated bonds of inner fulfillment and invests them in the alluring, but fleeting, junk bonds of material sensual pleasures. Much like trying to fill a bucket while also punching holes in the side, the energy required to attain spiritual realization and happiness never reaches the top and simply runs out. This isn't to say we shouldn't enjoy life. To the contrary, the more we are able to govern ourselves, the more enthusiasm we'll have to participate fully in life's diverse offerings.

The center of divine perception mentioned above is part of a group most commonly known as chakras. They are energetic hubs within our spiritual anatomy responsible for distributing life force along the spinal cord. Whenever this energy or life force is dominant in any particular chakra, our consciousness assumes the quality corresponding to that center. For example, when energies are dominant in the reproductive center, awareness is mostly of a sexual nature. When energies are dominant in the heart region, awareness is primarily of love. Divine union occurs when energies are focused at the chakra situated on top of the brain.

Non-sensuality seeks to promote higher consciousness by preserving the vital energies that can be depleted through sensual indulgence. Just as a steady diet of chocolate isn't great for our health, whatever feels good may not always be best for us. Discrimination and understanding are necessary to make wise choices, ones for our lasting benefit. Regarding sexuality, the ultimate sensual experience, non-sensuality doesn't advise suppression of it, which can be psychologically harmful. It does, however, counsel moderation, conservation, and transmutation of energy through meditation and related practices. By so doing, that tremendous force can be harnessed for spiritual ends.

Non-greed

The fifth and last guideline of the first step is non-greed. It may seem similar to non-stealing but there are subtle distinctions. While non-stealing emphasizes not coveting because it places joy outside the Self, non-greed stresses being not attached to externals, even to that which rightfully belongs to you. This doesn't suggest being irresponsible or insensitive, but instead encourages freedom from a limiting personal identification with things. We've all met people who get really angry if their car has been touched. Such attachment to cars, or for that matter, careers, bodies, incomes, houses, or social status, severely restricts a broader sense of being. People become shackled by belongings or self-image and blind to their greater nature. The truth is we're none of these things. We are Spirit briefly residing in a body for a journey of awakening. Non-greed shatters the attachments which cloak inner awakening and frees the consciousness from all delusive entanglements. Only in such freedom can the soul reclaim its divine heritage.

Summary

Now let's consider the practical application of these five principles in a general way. Their power is found in daily use where righteous living can transform and uplift us.

Through such practice we become worthy to receive lasting happiness and inner freedom, the true bounty of the Self.

Non-violence cultivates optimal harmony in personal and professional relationships. By removing the venom from competitive interactions, it fosters the kind of qualities necessary for useful cooperation. In bottom-line terms, people appreciate being treated well and will respond far better to kindness and consideration than to cruelty.

The practice of non-lying helps people to realize their fullest potential. Living within a world of "shoulds" and "what ifs" decreases the ability to deal effectively with "what is." By removing false images from their consideration, people can focus their efforts clearly on attaining chosen goals.

Non-stealing in turn prompts action that's uncorrupted by wrong impulses. By trusting in the spiritual basis for life and the virtue of right action, individuals become free from the pangs of restlessness and insatiable desire.

Non-sensuality further cultivates success by governing the expenditure of energy wisely. Self-control truly enhances personal power, magnetism, and thus our potential for dynamic, creative living.

Finally, non-greed releases us from worrying about the results of our labors. Though effort and outcomes are important to any endeavor, attachment to them can crimp the flow of creativity necessary for success. True genius can only blossom in the still spaces of inspiration unencumbered by thoughts of "me" and "mine." It cannot thrive in the toxic residue of worry or self-importance that arise with egotistic attachment.

STEP TWO: FOSTERING HARMONY

This step contains the five "do's," the remaining fundamental guidelines for spiritual cultivation:

- Cleanliness
- Contentment
- Austerity
- Self-study
- Devotion

They represent positive ideals to embrace, positive attitudes to maintain which foster harmony and spiritual unity. These five guidelines redirect awareness to our inner domain and set invaluable parameters for how to think and act on a daily basis. They help remove the tarnish of wrong thinking and behavior that obscures the already-perfect Self within. Our soul's light is perpetual and divine, never dimmed, only hidden by acts of ignorance. Once these are removed, the Self is revealed anew and shines with holy luster.

Cleanliness

The first of the "do" guidelines is cleanliness. Most of us are familiar with the expression "Cleanliness is next to godliness." But the practice of cleanliness involves far more than taking a regular bath. It actually refers to cleansing the heart and mind of anything adverse to Self. When individuals no longer seek things of the world, they evolve to more spiritual pursuits. Material infatuation is replaced by yearning for the Divine. This movement towards Spirit is a natural by-product of our innate hunger for Home. Cleanliness frees us from physical and emotional imperatives. It allows us access to the undiluted spiritual joy and pure, selfless love arising from our center. A more fitting maxim for this virtue is "Blessed are the pure in heart for they shall know God."

Contentment

Next is contentment. A seemingly unpretentious goal, contentment is actually very prized and not so easily attained. Consider that the bulk of daily affairs is directed towards outer accomplishment. We work for comfort and security, sometimes out of passion. We often establish personal identities based on our social status and spend tedious hours trying to improve it. Contentment however, while not rejecting honest labor or social good, reminds us to be ever mindful of and anchored to our inner joy amidst life's dance of change. Our outer activities or social position, no matter how exciting, upsetting, or boring, can only reflect back to us what we already have within. Joy which seems to arise from some outer source is never an objective part of that source, but rather a reflection of our own capacity to feel joy. By not assigning lasting value to anything outside the Self, we attain contentment in spite of social pressures. We can enjoy who and what we already are. Free from such self-centered worry, we become able to interact on a daily basis with lightness, sensitivity, and compassion.

Austerity

Austerity, the third "do" principle, typically conjures nasty images of severe and dour living. Once understood, however, this quality becomes both admirable and respectable. Most of us realize that nothing worthwhile is achieved in life without some form of self-control and effort. We enjoy the success stories of people who've overcome hardships to become leaders in their fields. Even Picasso and Mozart had to cultivate exacting standards in order to reap the rewards of their genius. Austerity is central to accomplishment. It demands that we reject whatever distracts us from our goals and do that which brings success. Spiritually speaking, this involves practicing certain disciplines, physical and mental, which foster self-control, equanimity, and soul awareness. Fasting is an example of one practice many traditions have used for ages. It moves us beyond a bodily orientation to one of spiritual sensitivity and perception. Although the belly may initially grumble and the mind rebel, eventually an inner freedom arises. By prodding us past environmental conditioning and self-imposed limitations, austerity cultivates a self-mastery necessary for gaining spiritual freedom. Austerity, therefore, is valuable for building a life of wisdom, not of habit.

Self-study

The fourth principle, self-study, looks past form, intellect, and emotion to shatter the small ego shell. Yet it is not merely a mental exercise. It is a practice of clear inner perception that goes beyond thought. By removing limiting perceptions of mortality and finiteness, consciousness is free to expand in boundless Self-realization. A famous saint had followers do this by repeatedly asking themselves "Who am I?" He pushed them to look ever deeper within, to gaze into their eternal and divine depths. Jesus revealed his own self-study when he said it wasn't he that did his works, but the Father who worked through him. Self-study helps us transcend the mirage of who we seem to be and to experience the totality of who we actually are.

Devotion

The last and perhaps most important principle for us to cultivate is devotion. The purity of devotion necessary to attain Salvation was aptly demonstrated by the Lord Buddha in his sacred vow for Enlightenment:

> *"Beneath the banyan bough*
> *On sacred seat I take this vow:*
> *'Until life's mystery I solve,*
> *Until I gain the Priceless Lore,*
> *Though bones and fleeting flesh dissolve,*
> *I'll leave this posture nevermore.'"*

It has been said that in all creation the only thing for which God truly yearns is our love. Such love and dedication to the Divine is devotion. Devotion is the earmark of true spirituality. It is the demonstration of faith, the manifestation of deepest feeling, and the gateway to Divine Union. As St. Augustine said, "Our souls are ever restless until they have found their true home in Thee." Most human love is selfish, conditional, and darkly rooted in desire. Devotional love on the other hand is freely given. It purifies the heart, uplifts the consciousness, and magnetically draws divine grace to nourish the soul and give lasting illumination. While meditation and right conduct are necessary to develop spiritually, even these are sometimes done with a dry attitude. Devotion opens the heart giving real strength and power to spiritual practice through love. It is the supreme factor for attracting the celestial response.

Summary

Through cleanliness or purity of heart we develop healthy self-esteem, learn to give without expectation of reward, and appreciate life more freely and fully. Such inner freedom fosters genuine goodwill towards others and lets sincerity flourish amidst the many moral challenges of daily life.

A natural outgrowth of cleanliness is contentment. Since no superficial allure can possess the mind of one truly contented, all activity becomes governed by wise discrimination, a balanced disposition, and practical serenity. This generates righteousness and virtue.

Austerity then serves to channel noble aspirations into worthy accomplishments. Through it we learn to govern and direct our energies most efficiently for optimal personal success.

Self-study provides a wonderful ego tonic. Realizing that we are aspects and instruments of the Divine allows us to honor ourselves and others on a core spiritual level. This fosters both humility and freedom from limiting personality complexes.

And lastly, devotion is the quality which, like sugar, sweetens whatever it touches. True devotion can buffer us against much of the grit in life. It provides a gentle inner smile, gives daily inspiration, and intoxicates the heart with love. Ultimately it moves our little piece of existence much closer to the Infinite Spirit.

STEP THREE: BEING STILL

The ten guiding principles for spiritual development outlined in steps one and two provide a foundation for daily thought and behavior, a cornerstone for moving forward into the actual practice of meditation. The next and third step to spiritual union is simple but extremely important. It regards proper posture in life and meditation.

Correct posture is necessary because it facilitates inner stillness, a vital element on the path of wisdom. Through dynamic stillness we learn more about our divine nature and consequently move closer to lasting freedom.

When positioned properly for meditation, the crown of the head should remain flat, chin parallel with the floor, and

hands rest on the thighs, palms up, at the junction with the torso. Next, imagine the scalp being pulled gently up to the sky. This aligns the head, neck, shoulders, and spine.

Sustaining this posture may cause some initial back fatigue due to weak or unused muscles. To avoid this fatigue, keep the hips higher than the knees by sitting on a firm, thick cushion on the floor. If a chair is more comfortable, select one that's straight-backed and doesn't invite slouching. Slide to the front of either chair or cushion to keep your bottom lifted and general body position strong. Having correct alignment is ultimately very relaxing and healthy. Once used to it, any other position will feel uncomfortably cramped.

Occasionally people ask about practicing meditation lying down or standing upright. My response is that since meditation involves deep relaxation, most people either fall asleep during the former or can't let go enough with the latter. I recommend that meditation be done in a comfortable, seated, and upright position whenever possible.

Meditation requires physical and mental relaxation. Prolonged sitting can tempt the body to fidget and the mind to drift. Unless fully at ease, tightened muscles or mental restlessness will trigger unconscious movement. Needless to say, both detract from deep inwardness. Many people who think relaxation is easy will find the opposite to be true. Even when sitting or lying down, tensions often linger. Relaxation is an acquired skill, particularly in this day and age when anxieties abound. Fortunately, there is a very effective way to counter this tendency: gentle stretching. It releases pent up energy from the body and, by focusing on the effect of each stretch, brings calmness to the mind.

Classically speaking, a perfectly relaxed seated posture enables one to remain unmoving and undisturbed in meditation for three hours. This stillness is so important because of energy. Life force, like electricity, animates and sustains us on multiple levels. It moves through the body in subtle channels known as meridians in Chinese medicine, or nadis in East Indian traditions. The spine is the primary conduit for this current. Meditation lifts and focuses energy, and correct practice requires straight posture to avoid crimping the energy flow. In addition, total stillness helps the body conserve energy by reducing the metabolic and cardio-pulmonary activity associated with movement. With less metabolic waste entering the blood stream, less energy is expended purifying the body. More energy is then available for inner concentration.

In very deep meditative states, energy withdraws completely into the inner spine and brain. The breath and heart can stop in suspended animation while the meditator taps directly into the flow of universal life force. This is obviously a high level of attainment, but it does exist. Jesus referred to it obliquely when He said, "Man shall not live by bread alone, but by every word that proceedeth out of the mouth of God." (Matthew 4:4) "Word" is the life force, and "the mouth of God" is the portal by which energy enters the body. Saints like Therese Neuman, a stigmatist from Bavaria, demonstrated this spiritual reality to an astonishing degree by living actively for many years without taking either food or drink.

Ultimately, the most important feature of correct posture is that it allows the mind to receive those spiritual insights perceived only in perfect stillness. The mind can be likened to a vast lake, susceptible to winds of thought and waves of restlessness. When agitated it can't accurately reflect its surroundings. When perfectly tranquil, it mirrors the vast panorama of reality. Included in this awareness are the exceedingly subtle vibrations of spiritual truth that remain hidden from minds swirling in worldly agitation. Perhaps this is one reason why Eastern cultures have traditionally prized serenity, and the Bible advises, "Be still and know that I am God." (Psalms 46:10)

STEP FOUR: CONTROLLING ENERGY

Energy moves through our bodies via meridians or nadis, as I mentioned. Now let's look further into the nature of energy, its impact, and why control of it is so important. This forms the fourth step towards Self-realization.

Life energy is a universal, intelligent, divinely originating force dynamically related to our physical well-being, mental and emotional states, and spiritual consciousness. Dominion over life energy, and the systems through which it flows, allows us to cultivate Divine Union. Since that's the goal of meditation, the value of energy control becomes self-evident. Understanding how to do this begins with an exploration of certain energetic fundamentals. How does energy enter the body? Where does it go? What is its effect on us?

Yogic adepts discovered that life force enters our bodies through a subtle energy portal located at the medulla oblongata. From there it travels to the brain and is directed into two channels which border the spine. As primary arteries for circulating life force, they carry it to energy centers or chakras, which distribute it through lesser meridians. The latter bring this animating force to our faculties, thus providing a living relationship with the world.

Chakras

There are seven chakras which channel life force from the lowest anal region to the uppermost crown of the head. Each chakra influences a specific plexus on the physical nervous system which in turn governs our triune constitution. Whenever energy is predominant in a particular chakra, our mental state reflects the consciousness associated with that chakra.

The lowest, the **root chakra,** located in the anal region, rather predictably controls the physical function of elimination. Psychologically it governs animal-like instincts while also fostering higher qualities of being grounded, centered, and stable. The spiritual aspect of this center reflects mastery over the first five guideline principles or "don'ts." As for the energy/awareness relationship, there are many nuances to these matters. Nonetheless, when life force accumulates in this region, consciousness leans towards survivalist attitudes or brutish behavior.

The **second chakra**, situated in the genital area, governs physical reproductive functions, a mental capacity for change, and the spiritual practice of the second five guideline principles or "do's." While the first chakra is often associated with the earth element, this center is water-like. Persons whose energy concentrates in this region will have a prominent fluid nature. This can manifest positively as being readily adaptable to shifting circumstances, or negatively as being adrift.

The **third chakra** at the navel controls physical digestion, mental creativity, and spiritual self-control. It's associated with the element fire and gives rise to dynamic creativity and power. Martial artists draw upon this chakra for inner strength and balance. It is generally an influential zone because it provides great force for any course of action. Those with the fiery dispositions associated with the third chakra must be careful to avoid directing their energy towards negative ends.

The **fourth chakra** is very important. Located at the heart, it governs physical respiration, emotional balance, and the airy quality of love. Highly influential because of its spiritual potential, this chakra is a pivotal center for how love is expressed. Whereas the bottom chakras address matters of a worldly nature, the top three relate to divine consciousness. This isn't a criticism or judgment, just an energetic reality. We need healthy functioning in all chakras to be fully balanced beings. Nevertheless, whenever energy is gathered at the heart center, love is activated. That love, once awakened, can either be raised to the centers of spiritual expansion or be directed down into lower worldly chakras.

In the latter instance love characteristically becomes conditional, selfish, jealous, and fickle. This expression of love is like nine carat gold, better than nothing but filled with impurities. On the other hand, love raised to the higher chakras becomes increasingly refined and purified until it is 24 carat, Divine. This love is selfless, unconditional, and perfect in every aspect. Lifting the focus of our love upward fulfills the Biblical commandment, "Thou shalt love the Lord thy God with all thy heart." (Mark 12:30) It stimulates love's grandest expression and we blossom with it.

The remaining chakras still affect us physically and mentally but are most important for their spiritual impact. The **fifth chakra** at the throat governs physical speech, mental peace, and spiritual calm. Distinguishing between peace and calmness is subtle but significant. Peace is the negative counterpoint of calm. It arises whenever there's a lack of disturbance. When nothing distressful ruffles the waters of consciousness, that is peace. It can be a refreshing break from life's ups and downs, but after a time the lack of stimulus gets stale. Eventually any sensation, positive or otherwise, becomes a desirable alternative to the inevitable emotional monotony. Calmness, on the other hand, is a truly enduring positive quality. Buoyant and ethereal, it's the dynamic state underlying peace. Never dull, spiritual calmness is self-sustaining whether circumstances are hectic or peaceful, and consequently it is perpetually rewarding.

The **sixth chakra** also is dual-natured and it has two poles. The negative is situated at the medulla oblongata and governs the autonomic nervous system. It is host to the ego, our deluded identification with the physical body. Without ego, the soul realizes its true nature as spirit and regains its legacy of freedom. This is kindled at the spiritual eye center or positive pole located between the eyebrows. This point, most noteworthy as the seat of divine will and soul consciousness, also stimulates frontal lobe function of creativity, enthusiasm, and joy. By deep concentration here, the doorway to the seventh and highest chakra, the **crown chakra**, opens. Therein lays access to various states of superconsciousness and the experience of Divine Union. The crown center, when fully awakened, fulfills the purpose of earthly existence and heralds our final return Home.

Ultimately the essence of all religious practices, regardless of outer orientation, is to promote this ascension of consciousness. Every effort at prayer, devotion, or turning within, any invoking of a higher power or seeking a greater Self is a conscious or unconscious act of directing energy and awareness towards the Absolute or Godhead. That's what makes the practice of energy control ultimately so important: its capacity to induce higher states of consciousness. Through such exercises, the life force which normally circulates in the two peripheral channels is balanced, disconnected from sensory stimulus, and withdrawn from the body. The normal downward flow of energy is reversed and drawn into a subtle canal running directly up the spine. Energy ascends this canal, spiritually illuminating every chakra until cosmic consciousness is awakened at the crown center of divine perception.

During sleep we disconnect from the senses but go into realms of subconscious experience. An adept in the process uses energy control to switch on or off their sensory connection at will, while remaining fully conscious. Such mastery of life force eliminates sensory distractions and facilitates its optimal use, achieving spiritual harmony.

The key to such control resides in the breath. Energy movement and its effect on mental states is intimately connected to breathing patterns. Knowing this, breath can be applied to cultivate spiritual consciousness. A word of warning though. Certain energy exercises can harm the nervous system unless properly practiced and supervised. Especially if the meditator is untutored, these may blast too much energy up the spine causing severe nervous system damage. Consequently, the safest method for lifting life force uses gentle breath patterns combined with concentration.

Concentration plays an important role in energy control because it directs force to the place of focus. By concentrating on the 6th chakra/spiritual eye for example, a magnetic influence is created at that center which safely coaxes energy to that spot. It's magnetism is like that created by passing a current through a coiled wire, only in this case, it passes through our inner spine. As this occurs, energy is naturally disconnected from the physical senses leaving the meditator sensitive to spiritual perceptions without distraction. Based on scientific principles, energy control is the means to an end, not the end itself. These practices will enhance the experience of anyone who uses them wisely, and they can be applied to any spiritual regimen without doctrinal conflict.

STEP FIVE: BRINGING AWARENESS WITHIN

The fifth step towards Divine Awakening or perfect meditation involves the art of bringing awareness within. As explained in the last section, energy control is intended to reverse the normal downward flow of life force from the brain. Bringing energy inside interiorizes the consciousness and allows the senses to disengage from outer stimuli. In sleep this occurs naturally, when we slumber peacefully amidst great clamor. However, sleep is a movement into the subconscious. To attain the superconscious states of meditation, the skill of interiorization must be practiced while fully conscious, alert, and focused. Without this capability, the meditator remains subject to a constant stream of sensory distractions plus the various memories they evoke.

The importance of this becomes clear in the following scenario:

A woman sits to meditate hoping to plunge into exciting new spiritual terrain. Comfortable at last, she practices a few energy-control exercises until a certain inner poise and balance arise. Feeling ready and eager to go deeper within, she suddenly hears a commotion from the kitchen downstairs. A favorite pie is being pulled from the oven and its luscious aroma slowly wafts upstairs. Stealing into the meditation nook, the savory smells entice her nose and tease her stomach. Fond memories whimsically spring forth in the meditator's mind of crisp autumn air, lovely trees, and Grandma's Thanksgiving cooking. Pretty soon all noble effort at meditation has been replaced by an imaginary holiday feast! Such is the oft-enjoyable yet distracting power of sense and memory stimulation.

Internalizing energy and awareness become practical necessities for inner development. The freedom arising from such practice lets us focus uninterruptedly on the divine quest. Sounds great, but how is it done? The actual process is achieved gradually in conjunction with certain breathing and energy-control exercises. These serve to stimulate, calm, or balance energy currents in the body. During interiorization, our attention shifts to feel and follow this subtle flow of energy as it moves inward. The predominant sensation that arises is of increasingly deep, yet alert, relaxation. The closest example I can think of is an extremely refreshing nap. Feeling comfortably cocooned within the inner perimeters of the body, any effort at movement requires an undesirable re-animation of the limbs. One just doesn't want to budge!

Such inwardness, delightful as it is, can be taken further. As energy retreats deeper into the astral spine, we feel less of the physical body and more of the life force currents as they move. By deeper identification with them, awareness of the outer world continues to fade away, replaced by delicate, blissful inner sensations. Once void of external distractions, our collective energy can be fully applied to achieve pure concentration, the sixth stage of Self-realization. Through such concentration long-cherished spiritual goals are brought very close to completion.

STEP SIX: CONCENTRATION

The sixth step—true concentration—has two aspects, one negative, the other positive. The former involves disengaging thoughts, perceptions, and attention from things not of immediate concern. The latter places the now undistracted attention single-pointedly upon any desired subject. This process is made possible according to the practices discussed in the last two chapters: establishing mental balance through energy control and making life force abundantly available through interiorization. With a calm, unruffled mind and energy withdrawn from sensory outlets, mental focus is poised for use at maximum potential. This allows pure concentration to be established.

Focused awareness is absolutely necessary to get spiritual returns. Without it, meditative effort can never truly bear fruit. The reason concentration is essential isn't just that it directs energy to centers of spiritual awakening. Of equal importance is the principle that whatever we focus on, we become. The following story illustrates this concept:

> Once there lived a renowned spiritual master whose main disciple developed an affectionate fixation for their tame water buffalo. This disciple lavished affection on the beast bringing it special foods, singing to it, grooming it, and so forth. After weeks of this pleasantly excessive behavior, the master decided to take action. He led the disciple to a secluded room and left him there to relax and do nothing but think of the favored pet. The disciple gladly agreed to this welcome respite from daily chores. Several days passed, however, and he found himself feeling lonely and bored. The master hadn't asked him to leave the room yet, and in fact wanted him to remain a while longer. But he felt cut off from human contact. Food was even sneaked in while he slept. Given such dreary isolation, the disciple took refuge in contemplating the tame buffalo. Morning, noon, and night that is all he did to keep somewhat happy and occupied. Eventually all concern for everyday life fell away. He became engrossed in deeper and deeper thoughts of the buffalo. Days later the master returned. When asked how he felt, the disciple replied in a gruff voice, "I'm very cramped in this tiny room." Obligingly, the master

opened the door inviting him to come out. The disciple then bellowed, "My great horns are too large for this puny door." The master smiled and mystically dispelled his disciple's concentration-induced perceptions. Having become so focused on the pet, the disciple developed buffalo-consciousness! The master then initiated him in a meditation technique where, with his now greatly augmented power of concentration, the disciple quickly achieved divine consciousness.

Creation is the manifestation of divine consciousness. Through concentration we assume the characteristics of whatever form it takes, be it buffalo or saint. The choice is ours.

Of the variety of concentration techniques available today, two are most frequently used. Both cultivate deep spiritual insight. The first, a form of mindfulness meditation, involves simply watching the breath—noticing it without controlling it. Because it requires no religious affiliation, this method is currently quite popular in the United States. By stopping restless mind chatter, it enhances inner clarity and perception of the Self. The practice utilizes breath watching to achieve final emancipation from delusion.

The second popular practice is more traditionally yogic in nature. It uses energy control, prayer, and devotional chanting to open the heart center. The mind, stilled by watching the breath, is then focused on divine manifestations like Jesus, Krishna, or Buddha, or on Spirit as love, light, sound, power, wisdom, peace, calm, joy. This method is closer to my heart because it evokes an intimate approach to God. Both practices, though different in flavor, produce similar states of concentration upon the Holy.

From a spiritually technical perspective, concentration taps into the very fundamentals of creation. Just behind the physical realm is one of energy or light, the astral universe. Behind that exists the more subtle causal universe of thought. Behind that is the domain of transcendent Spirit. Each soul is encased in a triune body of physical, astral, and causal elements. These form a sheath around the soul keeping it separate from God, like water floating in a bottle atop the ocean. Through concentration and meditation the cork to this bottle, spiritual ignorance, is pulled out, releasing the water, the soul, to freedom. This occurs for very specific reasons. Remember meditation is a spiritual science, not untested musings. By concentrating at the sixth chakra, a reflection of the medulla oblongata may be seen where con-

sciousness and energy enter the body. This spiritual eye appears as a five-pointed white star surrounded by a deep blue circle and golden halo. The blue light reflects the astral world, the gold light is of the causal sphere, and the white light is of Spirit. Through fixed attention, con-

sciousness can be projected through the white star into Spirit. After repeatedly diving into the Infinite, the soul drops its identification with the physical, astral, and causal sheaths and becomes one with the Cosmic Sea. In this manner concentration leads directly to oneness with Spirit.

STEP SEVEN: MEDITATION

Meditation is the seventh step on the journey to Self-realization. The distinction between meditation and concentration is both a matter of degree and context. While a person may concentrate on any subject they choose, proper meditation requires that such focus be directed singularly, exclusively on the Divine.

In true meditation there is no separation from the Divine. Consciousness becomes so completely absorbed in the object of spiritual focus that it is no longer distinct from it. Usually when people practice meditation, they are only concentrating deeply with the hope of attaining a meditative state. These aspirants may be totally concentrated on God or a divine attribute, but still have some residue of ego barring total spiritual immersion. Such a person, though fully focused on divine love, hasn't reached the point of becoming one with it. They remain separate, whereas the actual meditator has become divine love! Meditation is the complete immersion of individual human consciousness into Divine Consciousness. This leads to the final stage of Divine Union or Emancipation.

STEP EIGHT: DIVINE UNION

Self-realization, the awakened experience of oneself as Spirit, has been defined by a great early 20th-century master, Paramhansa Yogananda, as "the knowing—in body, mind, and soul—that we are one with the omnipresence of God; that we do not have to pray that it come to us, that we are not merely near it at all times, but that God's omnipresence is our omnipresence; that we are just as much a part of Him now as we ever will be. All we have to do is improve our knowing."

Divine union, also known as Self-Realization, is the eighth and final stage of Divine Awakening and follows naturally from meditation. Having gained the ability to direct life force into Cosmic Spirit, the meditator enters a trance state wherein awareness mingles with Spirit. By continual immersion in this expansive ecstasy, consciousness merges with the universal body of God throughout all creation. This achievement, called Sabikalpa Samadhi in the East, is also known as the attainment of Christ Consciousness. Yet higher states than this exist. In Nirbikalpa Samadhi, the most advanced level of cosmic consciousness, the soul unites with God both in creation and beyond. At this stage no bodily trance is exhibited whatsoever. One acts normally yet retains cosmic awareness. A saint of this stature when asked why he occasionally walked shakily replied that as he was in so many bodies at once it was sometimes hard recalling which to control!

Although such attainment seems far removed from our daily life experience, it represents our truest nature and grandest potential. That we can't readily conceive of this reality—much less pursue it—reflects the level to which our divine vision has become obscured. An appropriate analogy is that of a caged bird. From its perspective the limited quarters of captivity feel normal and safe. If the cage door were opened the bird would stay inside, fearful of the unknown. Even after venturing outside, it would return for security. Finally trusting its limitless freedom, the bird would soar away into the skies. We're the same way. After lengthy identification with the body cage, we grow tired of earthly disappointments and constraints. Seeking truth and freedom through spiritual practice, we find that we are more than mere physical bodies. This revelation is truly exciting yet so radical that we return to the familiar cage of limitations. After repeated inner experience, we discover that our divine nature feels comfortable and we want nothing less. With the awareness that our truth and absolute fulfillment lie in Spirit, we drown in the sea of infinity only to wake up.

Establishing a Practice

One great thing about the universe is how it accommodates our level and need for growth. As we advance spiritually, the right lessons, insights, and teachers come to facilitate the natural sequence of our development. These experiences, however, can be missed if we waste time comparing ourselves to others or expect to be on some level that we're not. It's not uncommon, for example, to want immediate gratification just because we've read about lofty spiritual states. While somewhat understandable, such a desire is really no more than spiritual materialism, an ego trip shifted to a spiritual playing field. The fact is that we don't know how far we've yet to travel on our journey nor when to expect a touch from the Divine. Even Jesus remarked that spiritual experiences come "like a thief in the night." Ignorant of when to expect them, we should nevertheless be vigilant to receive them. Thus it's best to simply begin the process and make haste slowly. Like anything else, spirituality takes time and perseverance to cultivate. So don't worry about outcomes, all the right seeds will grow in time. Constant fussing over them only kills the roots.

With all that said and done, let's examine the basics of how to begin a practice.

SPACE

The first thing needed is a space strictly for meditation. This can be a corner of a room or better yet, a separate room altogether. An altar of sacred objects like candles, incense, pictures of saints, or personal symbols of the Divine creates an uplifting, inspirational environment. They spiritualize the area. The late Joseph Campbell referred to such places as "sacred spaces," an appropriate term because that's precisely the theme of meditation. The reason for making a special area stems from the subtle power of vibrations. Every activity, thought, or word reflects a quality of consciousness and has a corresponding vibratory impact, much like the different rays of light on a spectrum. Dining rooms contain vibrations of meals and social eating, kitchens have those of cooking, and libraries of study. A space dedicated solely to meditation develops a vibration conducive to spiritual practice. Accordingly, no other activity should be conducted there. If family members or others share your space ask them to not disturb you while meditating, and if possible, arrange your practice schedule to avoid interruptions.

SITTING

The next thing you'll need to know is how to sit and what to sit on. Many people believe meditation requires painfully contorted postures, but thankfully such is not the case. In fact, whether on the floor or in a chair, comfort is the key. Discomfort has a nasty way of causing us to focus on aches and pains, when in actuality we need to forget the body in order to go beyond it. The only necessary condition for correct sitting is that the spine remain erect.

If you choose to sit on the floor, assume a comfortable cross-legged position atop a firm, thick, cushion. By elevating the hips and buttocks higher than the knees, the back is kept straight with minimal effort. If a chair is preferred, choose a simple straight-backed variety with a slender pillow on the seat. Sit away from the back of the chair with the feet uncrossed and flat on the floor. In either case, place the hands palms up at the junction of the torso and thigh. This hand position, though not absolutely mandatory, is definitely beneficial to inhibit slouching. Lastly, put a woolen blanket or silk cloth between your body and the ground. Silk or wool insulates against certain downward-pulling forces that oppose the uplifting efforts of meditation. Just as gravity holds us bodily to the earth, these forces act to keep our energies in the lower chakra centers of worldly consciousness. Insulating against them helps enhance our overall meditation practice. (See "Being Still," p. 58, for more information on sitting and posture.)

ALIGNMENT

Both alignment and time (see next section) are interesting concerns because they take into account the relevance and impact of nature. Some people feel that since meditation deals primarily with inner domains, external issues aren't important. Yet many groups including Native Americans, Indian Yogis, and Chinese Taoists have long valued being in tune with nature. They've understood that the earth operates according to complex natural forces, and by aligning ourselves to these subtle laws we cultivate a harmonious relationship with our broader Self. Nature, after all, is the grand body of God and it behooves us to pay Her close attention. Each direction, therefore, has meaning, purpose, and spiritual significance.

Yogis have traditionally suggested facing East or North for the best results in meditation. Energetic currents of enlightenment are said to flow from the East, while those of liberation issue from the North. Exactly why this is I can't say, but from my personal experience over the years I've been able to feel a difference when seated one direction or another. Of course, it's better to meditate facing any direction than to skip a session because a compass isn't handy.

TIME

The other concern of "natural" significance is what time is best to meditate. Classically speaking, four periods are ideal—dawn, noon, dusk, and midnight. These weren't arrived at arbitrarily, but reflect the impact of solar gravitational forces coupled with subtle energetic influences. Collectively these forces help restore balance to our own energy cycles. At noon the predominant impact comes from alignment to the sun's gravity. Just as many women claim the moon affects their monthly cycles, the sun has daily impact on us all. It's merely a matter of paying attention. Dawn and dusk are times of obvious transition, ones with a calmness which virtually anyone can feel. And finally, late night produces profound stillness. In fact, many people do their most creative work or have deepest meditations during the late night hours. One reason for this is that while everyone is sleeping the atmosphere is less cluttered from thought vibrations. This fosters astute mental clarity. For comparison's sake, pick a quiet place and try being creative or still during Monday morning rush hour traffic. Notice how you feel about the general atmosphere. Ultimately all four times are excellent, so select any two and make them regular practice periods.

Next comes the question of how long to spend in practice. For total beginners 15 to 20 minutes per session is sufficient, though 30 minutes would be better. For the restless or nervous, even this may seem enormous. Yet, as with anything else, practice makes perfect. The soul loves meditation, the ego doesn't. The deeper you go within, the more enjoyable the results. The less you practice, the easier it is to stop altogether. For those truly committed to meditation, three hours per day is a good standard to maintain. Finally, it's not the amount of time that's so important as the depth of your experience. It is better to go into Spirit for 30 minutes than to sit dozing for two hours!

Please note that distracting influences often mysteriously arise once you've decided to seriously embrace meditation. For some reason the Universe likes to play the trickster whenever someone strives to improve, especially spiritually. Be firm. Nothing is more important than your appointments with God. Remember, Christ said, "Seek ye first the kingdom of God, and His righteousness, and all these things shall be added unto you." (Matthew 6:33) Be sincere, be devoted, and practice. Daily!

Beginning Practices

Having a seat insulated by silk or wool and an altar to the East or North, it's time to begin practicing meditation in earnest. As you start, there are several things you'll want to do. First, keep your stomach relatively empty. A full belly uses energy for digestion when it should be directed towards alert, inner concentration. Secondly, sit on a chair or cushion, straighten your posture, and then relax comfortably. Keeping the back erect is necessary because a curved spine inhibits Self-Realization, but always remain at ease.

PRAYER

Now to begin. Pray. For those unfamiliar or rusty with this practice, the most helpful attitude for prayer is one of humility, devotion, and intimacy. Prayer should never be offered like a beggar before some icy, distant monarch. It should be simple, heartfelt and sincere, a loving demand to an infinitely compassionate parent, friend, or beloved. This kind of prayer isn't arrogant. Rather, it removes a sense of separateness and reflects our true belonging to God. So offer yourself into Spirit. Pray to know the Absolute. Then, with faith, be open to receive divine assistance and inspiration.

ATTITUDE

Next take some time to cleanse your attitude. As Jesus taught to make amends before going to pray, let go of your grievances. This action releases the hostilities which keep us feeling separate and uptight. In fact, all emotions, attachments, and desires should be surrendered to the Divine. This is a period of reverent focus. Worldly concerns can wait.

Be prepared to discount any false spiritual events such as theatrical hallucinations. The spiritual path is not a circus, but such episodes can occur, even if only rarely. Be aware that true superconscious vision comes from higher not lower consciousness. It inevitably evokes great joy and has a life-changing impact on those blessed to receive it.

Finally, learn to cultivate increasingly deep love and devotion for the Divine. Without these qualities no significant spiritual progress can be made, and meditation becomes wooden and hollow.

LETTING GO EXERCISES

Our next step is more physical in nature. To attain the profound stillness necessary for deep meditation, life force must be balanced and any remaining physical tensions must be dissolved. By using effective methods of achieving muscular release, results can be felt immediately. Once these relaxation techniques become familiar, the more subtle energy sequence will be more effective. Don't worry about getting lost in details. I will outline it all in proper order. For now simply let go and enjoy.

Tension/Relaxation Exercise

1. Double inhale, short then long, through the nose. This sounds like "hih, hiiiih."
2. Hold the breath and tense the entire body until it vibrates.
3. Double exhale, short then long, through the mouth. This sounds like "huh, huuuuh."
4. Relax completely and feel.
5. Repeat 3 to 6 times.

This exercise works wonderfully for a couple of reasons. First, many people don't relax well even in sleep because of hidden anxiety. Their stress manifests as energy accumulation, tension, which stays stuck in the body until accessed and released. Untreated, such toxic stress often leads to chronic health problems. By consciously tensing and relaxing the body, the lodged shards of energy loosen and reenter the system as available reserves for meditative or other purposes. Secondly, double breathing augments this process by drawing in fresh oxygen and dispelling carbon dioxide, too much of which impedes going deeply within. Together, both breathing and mindful tension help eliminate two obstacles to inner stillness and meditative discovery.

A wonderful complement to the above exercise is a more delicate technique using guided visualization and breath to mentally scan the body for tension.

Mental Scanning Technique

1. Begin visualizing the feet. Imagine space or openness entering into them with inhalation.
2. Exhale. Feel tension flow out and heaviness or warmth remain.
3. Repeat steps 1 and 2 for the ankles.
4. Now do the rest of the body: legs, thighs, pelvis, torso, upper arms, forearms, wrists, hands, shoulders, neck, throat, and head.
5. Inhale space, exhale tension. Each part should feel heavy or warm.
6. Repeat whenever tense or stiff.

ENERGY CONTROL EXERCISES

Knowing that energy flows through us linking together body and mind, we've utilized the flow to effect physical release through tension and relaxation exercises. Now let's take it to the more subtle level of energy control, where energy impacts the mind. The basis for this relationship lies in the breath-energy dynamic. In brief, breathing affects energy flow which in turn impacts brain activity. Have you ever noticed how you breathe when calm or excited? The rhythm, depth, and rate differ considerably. Likewise, have you ever tried to collect yourself by taking a few deep breaths? Whether you know it or not, such actions constitute a form of energy control.

In the science of energy control called pranayama, researchers have established that certain breathing patterns have very specific results. For example, breathing in the right nostril is said to stimulate left brain functions. Conversely, breathing through the left nostril affects the right half. A prescribed mixture of such breathing balances the energy in both brain hemispheres yielding mental stability and calm. With increasingly sensitive practice and expertise, advanced energy control naturally interiorizes consciousness by withdrawing life force from the sensory-motor system. For our purposes we shall concentrate on the most important first step in this process: calming the mind. The two exercises that follow accomplish this goal very safely and effectively. Yet even these techniques should not be trifled with nor overdone. Practice each until you get the hang of them. Once familiar with how they feel, choose which to use and when.

The first technique is a very simple breath regulation process.

Energy Control Exercise #1

1. Close your eyes.
2. Inhale through the nose for a count of 8 or 10 or 12. Do whatever is comfortable.
3. Hold the breath for an equal time.
4. Exhale through the nose for the same duration.
5. Repeat steps 2, 3, and 4 three to six times safely.

To enhance the technique, imagine inhaling calmness into the brain. Hold that breath and feel the mind bathed in peace. Exhale and melt into tranquillity.

The second exercise, Alternate Nostril Breathing, has a more intricate breathing pattern. I recommend practicing the first exercise twice daily for two to four weeks before starting the second exercise.

Energy Control Exercise #2: Alternate Nostril Breathing

1. Close your eyes.
2. Start by isolating the thumb and ring finger of the right hand.
3. Place the right thumb gently over the right nostril closing that air passage.
4. Inhale through the open left nostril for a comfortable count.
5. Lightly pinch both nostrils closed with thumb and ring finger. Hold the breath for an equal count.
6. Release the right thumb, keep the left nostril closed.
7. Exhale through the right nostril for the same count.
8. Without switching finger positions, inhale through the right nostril.
9. Lightly pinch both nostrils closed with thumb and ring finger. Hold the breath for an equal count.
10. Release the right ring finger, keep the right nostril closed.
11. Exhale through the left nostril for an equal count.
12. Repeat steps 3 through 11 three times. (In left, hold, out right—In right, hold, out left = one cycle. 3 cycles are perfectly safe.)

CONCENTRATION TECHNIQUES

Following the calming of mind and body, energy must be directed to where it will lift our consciousness towards the Divine. To accomplish this, simply close the eyes and gently gaze up to the point between the eyebrows known as the spiritual eye or sixth chakra. Look within as though down a tunnel or telescope. If there's any discomfort it usually stems from lack of practice or trying too hard. Just relax. Place the eyes effortlessly like light beams on a wall, never crossed nor strained. If the gaze still feels awkward, don't fret. It will naturally roll upwards as consciousness is raised.

Correct eye placement at this center is extremely important. The eyes emit a subtle electrical current that stimulates and opens the door to higher spiritual awareness. From this center of divine will within us our consciousness and thoughts can be directed into Spirit.

With the gaze directed at the spiritual eye, it's time to learn a classical technique designed to induce deep concentration. This particular technique uses what's called a mantra. A mantra is a word, phrase, or sound of spiritual power. Such words or sounds have the vibrational capability to induce definite physical, mental, or spiritual states. Sound is vibration which has greater or lesser degrees of force depending on its use. Everyone knows the power of sound vibrations to shatter glass, summon dogs, or cause avalanches. This principle is simply applied spiritually.

From a spiritual context, words are important because they reflect the vibrations of different states of consciousness. The term "love," for example, has a vibration different from that of "rage". Every word has qualities setting it apart from other sounds. To focus the mind, it is beneficial to use vibrations which produce a state of concentration.

The method you are about to learn is an ancient but well-known practice. It combines the practice of watching the breath with the repetition of two words derived from Sanskrit, "Hong Sau," also frequently called "Hum Sa" or "So Hum." These words mean "I am He," or, "I am Spirit." What's most important is the power they convey to facilitate concentration, calming of the heart. Through the Hong Sau mantra, normal breathing is slowed down— sometimes even stopped. The energy used for cardio-respiratory and related metabolic processes is then withdrawn from the physical body and made available for pure concentration by gazing into the spiritual eye.

While of Eastern derivation, this technique only induces concentration, it doesn't imply a specific religion. It can be practiced regardless of belief system. Other traditions sometimes use similar methods to deepen inner experience. The Russian Orthodox, for example, recite the classic "Jesus prayer" ("Lord Jesus Christ, have mercy on me/us") in an identical breath or prayer formula. Dr. Herbert Benson, a Harvard cardiologist and author of *The Relaxation Response*, tested various disciplines to measure their body-mind impact. He found that when simple word sets, either secular or religious, were repeated in conjunction with mindful breathing, extremely relaxed mental and physical states resulted. However, I believe that the spiritual component of word formulas does add a definite quality not found in those of secular design.

Whether you use Hong Sau, Hum Sa, the Jesus Prayer, or a personally meaningful word set, the breath-sound technique is practiced the same. Notice in the following exercise that the order of tension/relaxation and energy control techniques has been reversed. This is the correct way to practice. Other focus words can be substituted for "Hong Sau".

Concentration Technique

1. Sit facing east, close the eyes and gently lift them to the spiritual eye center.
2. Begin with a prayer of your choosing.
3. Use either Energy Control Technique. (p.85, p.86) Be alert to feel the results.
4. Practice the Tension/Relaxation exercise. (p. 83) Concentrate on the calm after-effects.
5. Take a deep breath in through the nose. Exhale quickly without any regulation.
6. Stay without breathing for as long as comfortable.
7. When ready, observe the breath flow in and out of the nose. Don't control it, simply be aware.
8. Next, as breath enters the nostrils mentally repeat "Hong" (like "song").
9. As breath leaves the nostrils, mentally repeat "Sau" (like "saw").
10. With each inhale/exhale, watch the breath repeating "Hong-Sau" as described.
11. Practice accordingly for 10–30 minutes.
12. Release the breath slowly, emptying the lungs. Hold out as long as comfortable.
13. Enjoy this breathless state. Repeat several times.
14. Forget the breath and pray, or remain in complete stillness and peace.

Keep the following points in mind while practicing the concentration technique:

1. The breath must never be forced to conform to any rhythm or expectation. There are times when it flows in differing lengths or remains out for various durations. Let it be. The goal is to watch the breath and let that have a calming effect upon the heart.

2. Enjoy the periods of non-forced breathlessness when the ego loses attachment to breathing. Realizing the body is sustained only partially by breath, the soul gradually releases its identification from the body. Concentrate upon those intervals.

3. Breathlessness and corresponding internal organ relaxation disconnects energy from the senses. Thus freed from sensory intrusion and subconsciously aroused thoughts, the mind can concentrate completely upon God. Such concentration becomes meditation.

MEDITATION PROCESS

Through meditation we become attuned to Spirit, and only by such attunement do we realize Oneness with God. The method we'll use to achieve this harnesses the concentrated mind, prayer, and receptive inner "listening." As mentioned earlier, the sixth chakra is both the seat of divine will within us and a broadcasting station for our thoughts. By consciously directing heartfelt prayers from this center to Spirit, we activate the process of establishing divine communion. Begin knocking on the door to the Infinite by summoning love or longing from the heart. Lift this soul call to the spiritual eye, then project it out to God in the simple, personal language of love. St. Francis of Assisi did

so by praying "My God and my all" until Jesus appeared to him. A certain Hindu saint cried "Reveal Thyself" or "Come to me" until God filled him with spiritual ecstasy. It's ultimately such devotional prayers that move the Divine to respond.

Following a period of ardent prayer, keep gazing into the spiritual eye but let your attention drop to the heart center where celestial response is usually felt. Wait patiently, neither tense nor grasping, for a reply. Whatever comes, become absorbed in it. Some may see an inner light or hear celestial music. Others might receive tremendous peace, calm, love, or joy. Of all things, be mindful of a joy that floods the heart. Such joy is held to be the surest sign of God's reply.

Regardless of the manifestation, contact with an aspect of the Divine has been made. By deeper meditation the soul resonates like a tuning fork in perfect harmony with a higher frequency, Spirit. Consciousness then expands, melting into and permeating the cosmos in triumphant union with the Divine. With this achievement comes the crowning victory of complete Self-Realization. The glorious purpose of meditation is fulfilled. For a marvelous rendering of this phenomena read the poem "Samadhi" by Paramhansa Yogananda in *Whispers From Eternity* or *Autobiography of a Yogi*.

Meditation Procedure

1. Begin with a prayer.
2. Practice the preparatory Tension/Relaxation and Energy Control exercises.
3. Practice the Concentration Technique for 10–30 minutes.
4. Period of prayer demands or soul calls.
5. Receptive inner listening.
6. Go deeper. Become absorbed in the response.
7. Expand into complete Divine Union.

CONCLUSION

The question remains how to translate such lofty experience into practical life. There are no pat answers. When all is said and done, it's not just what is gained personally that makes meditation so attractive, but also what is shared collectively. Because meditation impacts our ways of thinking, perceiving, and reacting, we influence the lives of others with whom we come in contact. By changing ourselves we make the world a better place. The contribution may be subtle, but it's real. Being a positive force in family, business, and social life is so needed in these critical times. Be a power by which many are lifted.

The sacred journey is a process. It takes time and committed effort, so don't rush. Above all, don't quit. Illumination is real and attainable. If your experience isn't cosmic, or is fairly uneventful, don't worry about it. Be content and remember what Jesus said, "Ask, and it shall be given you; seek and ye shall find; knock, and it shall be opened unto you." (Matthew 7:7) Consider that at the end of your days what you earn stays here, but what you learn goes beyond. Plant seeds of spiritual aspiration in the soil of meditation. Water them with faith, devotion, and practice. Then surely will the harvest bear divine fruit.

Glossary of Terms

Astral Subtle life energy, finer than that of the physical realm.

Causal Behind the physical, material world and the energetic, astral realm, the world of thought.

Chakras Seven centers of life force and consciousness located in the brain and spine which empower both the physical and energetic or astral body.

Christ Consciousness The state of universal consciousness or oneness with God within all creation.

Cosmic Consciousness The state of absolute consciousness, or oneness with God within and beyond all creation.

Disciple One who comes to a master seeking to know God.

Guru An enlightened master capable of helping the sincere spiritual seeker, or disciple, fulfill his/her divine quest.

Karma The spiritual law of cause and effect, action and reaction. The divine law of justice.

Master One who has attained complete self-mastery as evidenced through Self-realization.

Prana Essential force of life, astral substance.

Pranayama The science of consciously controlling life force or prana.

Samadhi The highest stages of God-communion wherein the meditator's consciousness merges with Infinite Spirit. (The sabikalpa samadhi state is fixed, trance-like. The nirbikalpa samadhi state is without any bodily fixation). Self-realization.

Self Capitalized, refers to the soul, as opposed to the self, or individual ego personality.

Soul An individualized aspect of Spirit.

Spiritual Eye The sixth chakra, portal to ultimate states of spiritual awareness.

Superconsciousness The perfect, pure consciousness of the soul.

Yoga The spiritual science of attaining divine union.

Yogi Anyone who practices a scientific method of realizing God.

Bibliography

Arnold, Sir Edwin. *The Song Celestial*. Wheaton, Il: Theosophical Publishing House, 1970.

Benson, Herbert. *The Relaxation Response*. New York: William Morrow, 1975.

Dossey, Larry. *Healing Words: The Power of Prayer and the Practice of Medicine*. New York: HarperCollins, 1993.

Evans-Wentz, W. Y. *Tibet's Great Yogi Milarepa*. London, England: Oxford University Press, 1928.

Kabat-Zinn, Jon. *Full Catastrophe Living: Using the Wisdom of Your Body and Mind to Face Stress, Pain, and Illness*. New York: Delacorte, 1991.

M. *The Gospel of Sri Ramakrishna*. New York: Ramakrishna-Vivekananda Center, 1942.

Osborne, Arthur. *The Teachings of Ramana Maharshi*. London, England: Century, 1962.

Prabhavananda, Swami and Christopher Isherwood. *How to Know God: The Yoga Aphorisms of Patanjali*. New York: Mentor, 1953.

St. Teresa of Avila. *Interior Castle*. Garden City, NY: Image, 1961.

Tweedie, Irina. *Daughter of Fire*. Nevada City, CA: Blue Dolphin Publishing, 1986.

Walters, J. Donald. *The Reappearance of Christ*. Nevada City, CA: Crystal Clarity Publishers, 1987.

Walters, J. Donald. *Rays of the Same Light*. Nevada City, CA: Crystal Clarity Publishers, 1988.

Yogananda, Paramhansa. *Whispers From Eternity*. Los Angeles, CA: Self-Realization Fellowship Press, 1935.

Yogananda, Paramhansa. *Autobiography of a Yogi*. Los Angeles, CA: Self-Realization Fellowship Press, 1946.

Yogananda, Paramhansa. *Man's Eternal Quest*. Los Angeles, CA: Self-Realization Fellowship Press, 1975.

Yogananda, Paramhansa. *The Divine Romance*. Los Angeles, CA: Self-Realization Fellowship Press, 1986.

Yukteswar, Swami Sri. *The Holy Science*. Los Angeles, CA: Self-Realization Fellowship Press, 1949.

Pocket Guides from The Crossing Press

Pocket Guide to Aromatherapy
By Kathi Keville
$6.95 • ISBN 0-89594-815-X

Pocket Guide to Good Food
By Margaret M. Wittenberg
$6.95 • ISBN 0-89594-747-1

Pocket Macrobiotics
By Carl Ferre
$6.95 • ISBN 0-89594-848-6

Pocket Guide to Naturopathic Medicine
By Judith Boice
$6.95 • ISBN 0-89594-821-4

Pocket to Self Hypnosis
By Adam Burke
$6.95 • ISBN 0-89594-824-9

Pocket Guide to Stress Reduction
By Brenda O'Hanlon
$6.95 • ISBN 1-58091-011-4

Pocket Guide to the Tarot
By Alan Oken
$6.95 • 0-89594-822-2

Pocket Guide to The 12-Steps
By Kathleen S.
$6.95 • ISBN 0-89594-864-8

Pocket Guide to Visualization
By Helen Graham
$6.95 • ISBN 0-89594-885-0

Pocket Guide to Wicca
By Paul Tuitean & Estelle Daniels
$6.95 • ISBN 0-89594-904-0

To receive a current catalog from The Crossing Press
please call toll-free, 800-777-1048.
Visit our Web site: **www.crossingpress.com**